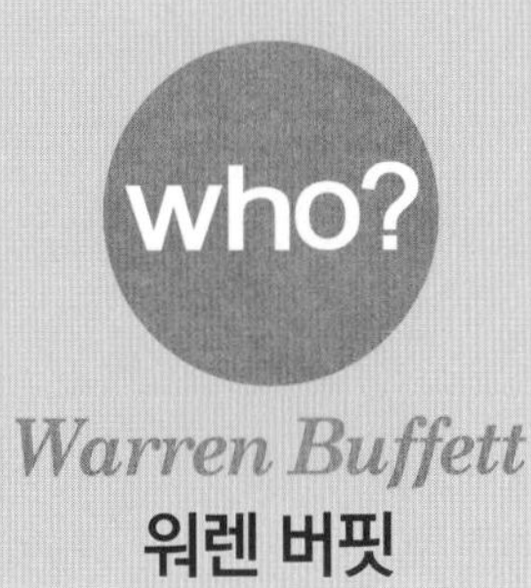

who?

Warren Buffett

워렌 버핏

Biography Comic
who? 16 Warren Buffett

개정판 1쇄 인쇄 2014년 3월 5일
개정판 1쇄 발행 2014년 3월 10일

글 오영석
그림 크레파스
번역 샐리 박
감수 김수희
펴낸이 김선식

책임편집 이유미 **디자인** 박효영
콘텐츠개발팀장 김선영 **콘텐츠개발팀** 박효영, 이유미, 김선민, 조서인
마케팅본부 이상혁

펴낸곳 스튜디오 다산 **출판등록** 2013년 11월 1일 제414-81-37694
주소 경기도 파주시 회동길 37-14 3층
전화 02-702-1724(기획편집) 02-703-1725(마케팅) 02-704-1724(경영관리)
팩스 02-703-2219 **who클럽** cafe.naver.com/dasankids
종이 월드페이퍼(주) | **인쇄** (주)현문 | **제본** 광성문화사

ISBN 979-11-5639-008-4 (14740)

글 **오영석** | 그림 **크레파스** | 번역 **샐리 박** | 감수 **김수희**

Dasan Kid

Warren Buffett

Entrepreneur, August 30, 1930 ~ present

The top investor of the twenty-first century, Warren Buffett was born in 1930 in Omaha, Nebraska, in the U.S. He loved numbers ever since he was young. When he was six years old, he would buy gum and soda at his grandfather's store and sell it for a profit.

As Warren saved up money and became interested in watching the numbers get bigger, his father helped him start investing in stocks. He learned the "value investment" theory, which says to invest in a company's potential and future value after carefully investigating it for a long time and watching how the stock market is flowing. At the age of eleven, he invested in stocks for the first time and made a weekly profit of three dollars.

During his teenage years, Warren enjoyed delivering newspapers. Unlike other delivery boys, he divided up his area systematically so that he could deliver a large number of newspapers in the shortest amount of time. His ability to devise such a plan resulted in him having a larger salary than an adult.

Warren studied business in college, as his father desired. He then went on to Columbia Business School and studied under Benjamin Graham, the first proponent of value investing. After graduating, Buffett took his first steps as a full-fledged investor by forming an investment partnership which became very profitable. At the young age of thirty-two, Buffett joined the ranks of the millionaires.

During his work with investment partnerships, he bought the stocks to a faltering business called Berkshire Hathaway and gained control of the company. Afterwards, he dissolved his very profitable investment partnerships and began investing in Berkshire Hathaway. Because of his successful investment activities, he was selected by Forbes magazine in 2008 as the world's richest man in the world.

After enjoying great wealth, Warren Buffett realized that simply holding onto money kills its worth. Consequently, he announced that he would give more than half of all of his money to society. Even today, he leads a happy wealthy life as he shares his wealth with people in need.

워렌 버핏

기업가, 1930년 8월 30일 ～

21세기 최고의 투자가 워렌 버핏은 1930년 미국 오마하에서 태어났습니다. 워렌 버핏은 어릴 적부터 숫자 모으기를 좋아했습니다. 6살 때에는 할아버지의 가게에서 산 껌과 콜라에 이윤을 붙여 사람들에게 팔기도 하였지요.

조금씩 돈이 모이고, 숫자가 커지는 것에 흥미를 느낀 그는 아버지의 도움으로 주식 투자를 시작합니다. 오랜 시간 신중하게 회사를 조사하고, 주식의 흐름을 지켜본 후, 그 회사가 가진 가능성과 미래의 가치에 투자하라는 '가치 투자'이론에 감명을 받은 워렌 버핏은 11살에 처음으로 주식에 투자하여 주당 3달러의 이윤을 냅니다.

청소년 시절, 워렌 버핏은 신문 배달에 재미를 붙였습니다. 다른 배달부들과는 달리 구역을 체계적으로 나누어 가장 빠른 시간에 많은 신문을 배달할 수 있는 방법을 고안한 그는 능력을 인정받아 어른보다 많은 월급을 받게 됩니다.

워렌 버핏은 아버지의 뜻에 따라 대학에서 경제학을 공부하였고, 컬럼비아 경영 대학원에 들어가 가치 투자의 창시자로 불리는 벤저민 그레이엄의 제자가 됩니다. 대학원을 졸업하고 본격적인 투자자의 길로 들어선 그는 자신의 이름을 건 투자 조합을 만들어 큰 이윤을 냅니다. 그리고 32세의 젊은 나이에 백만장자의 대열에 들었습니다.

워렌 버핏은 투자 조합의 활동 중 스러져가던 기업인 버크셔 헤서웨이의 주식을 사들여 경영권을 얻었습니다. 그 후, 높은 수익률을 내던 투자 조합을 해체하고 버크셔 헤서웨이의 이름으로 투자를 시작합니다. 그리고 성공적인 투자 활동을 하여 2008년에는 경제지 '포브스'가 선정한 세계 최고의 부자가 되었습니다.

큰 부를 누리고 나자 워렌 버핏은 돈을 가지고만 있는 것은 그 가치를 죽이는 일이라는 것을 깨닫게 됩니다. 그래서 자신이 가진 돈의 절반 이상을 사회에 기부하겠다고 선언합니다. 오늘도 그는 자신의 부를 어려운 사람들과 나누며 행복한 부자의 길을 걷고 있습니다.

글 · 오영석

어린이들이 재미있고 신나게 읽을 수 있는 책을 쓰기 위해 노력하는 작가입니다. 나와 똑같이 고민하고, 실패했던 위인들의 이야기를 통해 독자들도 '할 수 있다'는 마음을 가지길 바랍니다. 작품으로『세계사 한국사』,『과학 교과 주제 탐구Q. 몸』,『걸어서 세계 속으로 2. 일본』등이 있습니다.

그림 · 크레파스

어린이들을 위해 새롭고, 재미있고, 즐거운 이야깃거리를 만드는 만화 창작 집단입니다. 세상을 바꾼 인물들의 삶을 통해 어린이들이 희망찬 미래를 만들어가길 바랍니다. 작품으로 『지식 똑똑 경제 리더십 탐구-긍정의 힘』,『why? 서양 근대 사회의 시작』,『why? 세계대전과 전후의 세계』등이 있습니다.

번역 · 샐리 박(Sally Park)

캐나다 토론토에서 태어나고 미국 뉴저지 주에서 자랐습니다. 유치원부터 중학교까지 한글학교를 다니고 졸업했습니다. 현재 뉴저지 주립대학교인 럿거스에서 영어와 심리학을 전공하고 있으며, 어린이책을 번역하고 있습니다.

감수 · 김수희

연세대학교에서 역사를 전공했습니다. 이후 한국뿐 아니라 일본, 미국에서 한국어, 일본어, 영어를 가르쳐 왔으며 부모를 위한 영어교육용 책을 썼습니다. 영어교육채널 EBSe '엄마표 영어특강'에서 강의를 하며 홈스쿨, 알파벳과 파닉스, 다차원 테마 영어 수업 기법을 알리고 있습니다. 전국 각지에서 어린이 영어 교육에 대한 강연을 하며 창의적이고 열정적인 교수법으로 영어를 배우고자 하는 어린이와 부모들에게 많은 도움을 주고 있습니다.

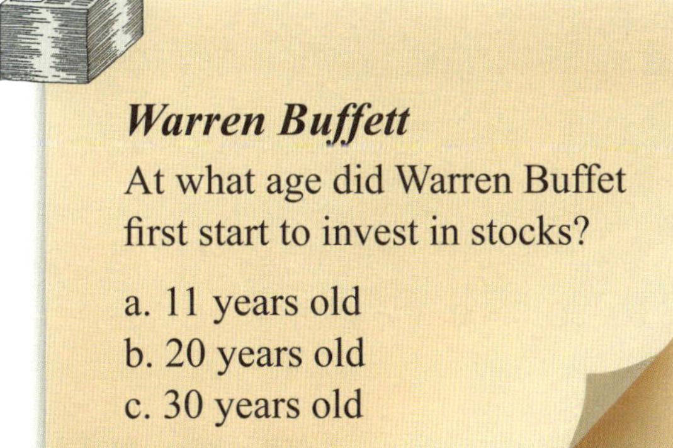

Contents

01 The Boy Who Likes Numbers

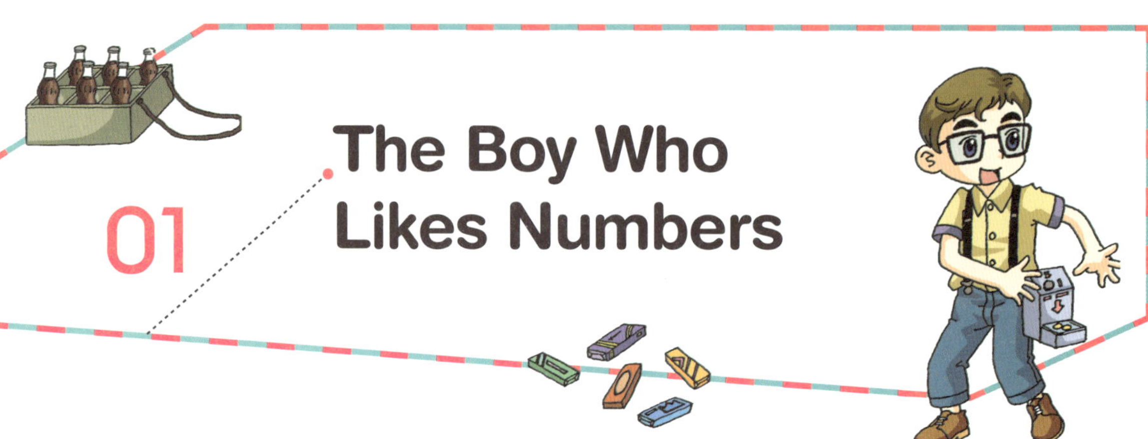

This young boy, who was born in the year 1930, really enjoyed pretending that he was a merchant.

The boy's older sister, Doris, did not understand why.

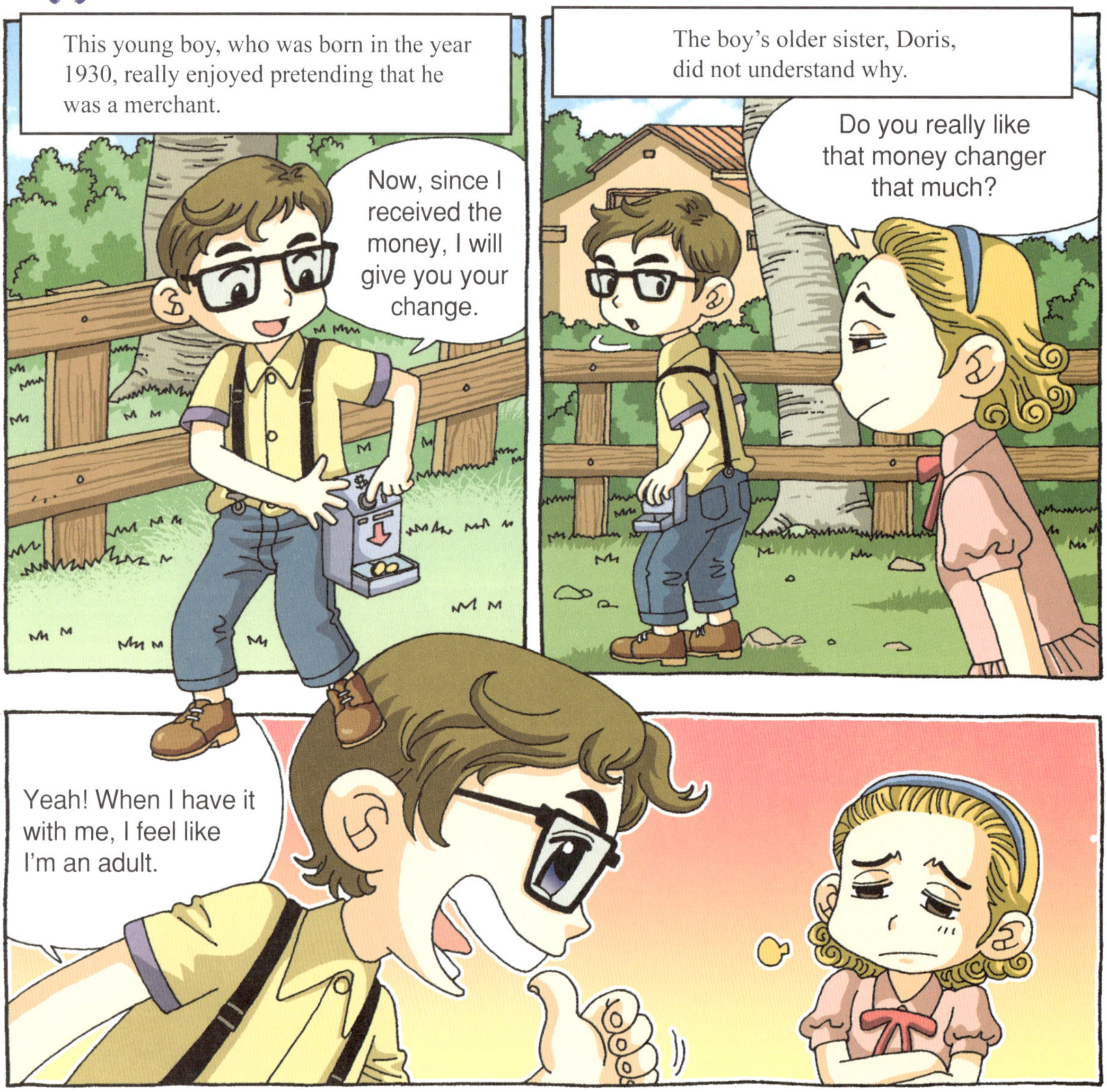

This young boy also liked to play with his stopwatch.

Okay, ready?
PLOP

CLICK
Start!

Yes! Contestant Rock made it to the finish line in 1 second and 48 milliseconds.

It's a new record!
Warren, you're so loud! Be quiet!

Doris, this person lived until 76 years of age. That's a pretty long life.
So what?

But this other person lived a very short life and died at age 36.
Why on earth are you telling me all of this?
This boy loved numbers and dividing things based on classification.
There's no special reason. I just thought I'd divide them into two groups: people who live long and people who don't.
This boy is Warren Buffett, and he will grow up to become one of the richest men in the world.

BUFFETT MARKET
BUFETT MARKET

OPEN

Hi and welcome... Oh Warren, is that you?
SALE

Yes, Grandpa. I came to visit you.

Warren, I haven't seen you in a while. Do you want something tasty to eat?
HAM

What are you saying? Nothing in this world is for free.
Oh, yes. I'm sorry, boss.

Warren, whenever you want to eat something, you need to pay for it. You need to pay a fair price for the items you want.
Yes, I know. That's why I brought the money that I had saved up.

I would like some packs of gum, please.

Packs? Why so many?
I want to do business, too.

Business?

In order to sell the gum he had bought from his grandpa's store, Warren went out onto the street. Because Warren loved numbers, he wanted to be able to collect them. In fact, he wanted to collect these beloved numbers in the form of money.
Buy gum! Buy gum!
Hey kid! I'd like a pack of gum.
The price of the gum is one cent higher than it is at the store.
What? Why?
Because now you won't have to go all the way to the grocery store for a pack of gum.

Warren sold his gum for a little more than what it costs at the grocery store. However, people who didn't want to walk to the store for gum, gladly bought it from Warren.

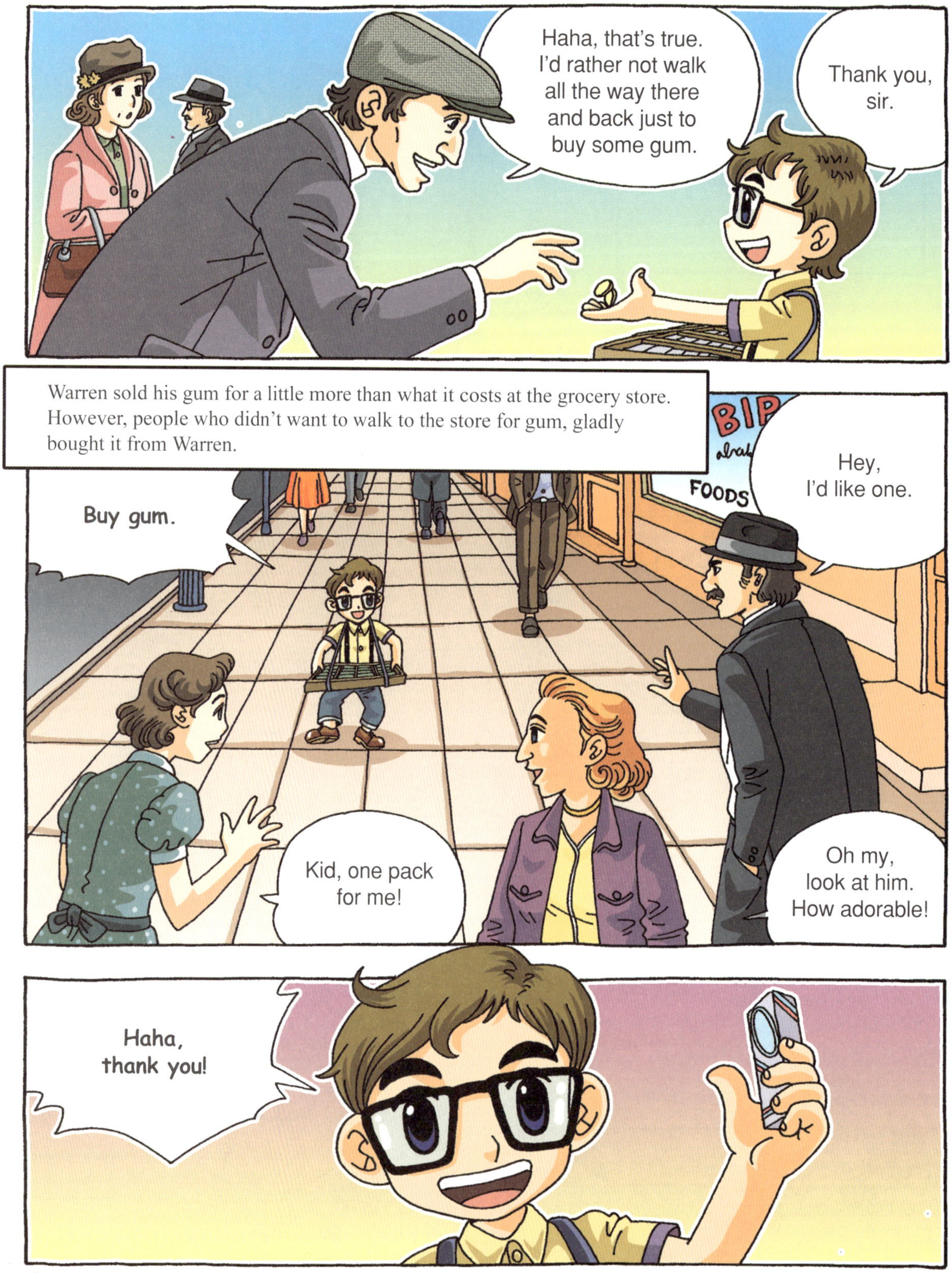

Kids, your father's home!
Hello, father.

Oh, my little princess. How are you doing today? You didn't fight with your little brother now, did you?

Hi, honey.
Hi, sweetie. Where's Warren?

Well, he's been doing something in his room for a while now. He's always been a silly child.

This kid. Daddy comes home and you don't even come out to see me?
Oh, Dad!

But, wait...

What are you doing?

I'm dividing the bottle caps that I collected into groups based on the different types.

Based on types? Why?

I wanted to know what drink was selling the best.
These two are both Coke bottle caps but I see you've divided them up.

Ah, it's because they're different! One of them was sold from a vending machine.

I had to separate them because this side is for bottle caps from drinks that were sold in stores.
But why are you collecting bottle caps?

I want to find out which drink people like better and start selling it.
Sell it? Aren't you selling gum these days?

Yes, but the gum isn't selling as well as I thought it would. I'm thinking about selling something else now.
What are you going to sell this time?
From now on, I'm going to sell Coca-Cola.

Coke? You want to sell Coke?

Yes. I realized that more people buy Coke than gum.
APPLE JUICE
TOMATO KETCHUP
JUICE
SALE 10% OFF
Since Coke is 25 cents for a box of 6 bottles, wouldn't it be okay if I sold each bottle for 5 cents?

Hmm, I don't think that's a good idea.
Why not?

When you sell a pack of gum, you make 1 cent. So, when you sell 6 packs of gum, you make 6 cents, right?
Yes.

But if you sell 6 bottles of Coke, you'd only be making 5 cents.

But the amount of people who buy Coke is way bigger than the amount that buy gum.

If 10 people buy gum from me in one day, I'll have 10 cents left over. If 20 people buy Coke from me in one day, I'll have 15 cents left over.

Ah, that is plausible.

Warren went around selling Coke instead of gum. There were more Coke buyers than there were gum buyers.

Buy some Coke. A bottle costs 5 cents.

Hey, give me a bottle of Coke.

Hey kid, a bottle here, too!

Oh good, I was so thirsty. Hey! I would like one, too.

Warren had put all the money he had raised in his desk drawer. As the amount of money he had increased in unit, the more money Warren wanted to collect.

Honey. About Warren...
Huh? What about Warren?

I'm a little worried because he's so young and so in love with money.

Haha. It's not the money he's in love with but the numbers. 1 cent becomes 10 cents, and cents add up to dollars, etc. He just enjoys watching the numbers grow.

But he also tries to spend more time with adults instead of playing with his peers...
Our son is like a ball of fire, burning bright with energy. Maybe there just isn't anyone among his peers that understands his kind of energy.

Either way, he's eventually going to grow up anyway so don't worry.

I'm glad...

I'm going to see what Warren's up to.

Hey Warren, what are you doing? I have a present...

Warren!

!

Leila, call the doctor! Warren must've fainted.
What happened?

The doctor arrived soon after and examined Warren.

Is he okay, doctor?

He has an extremely high fever. Now that he's been prescribed, you'll have to see how he progresses. If, however, his fever does not go down by tomorrow, it will be very dangerous to his health.

Oh, gosh!
No.

You mean... I could actually die?

How much money did I save up?

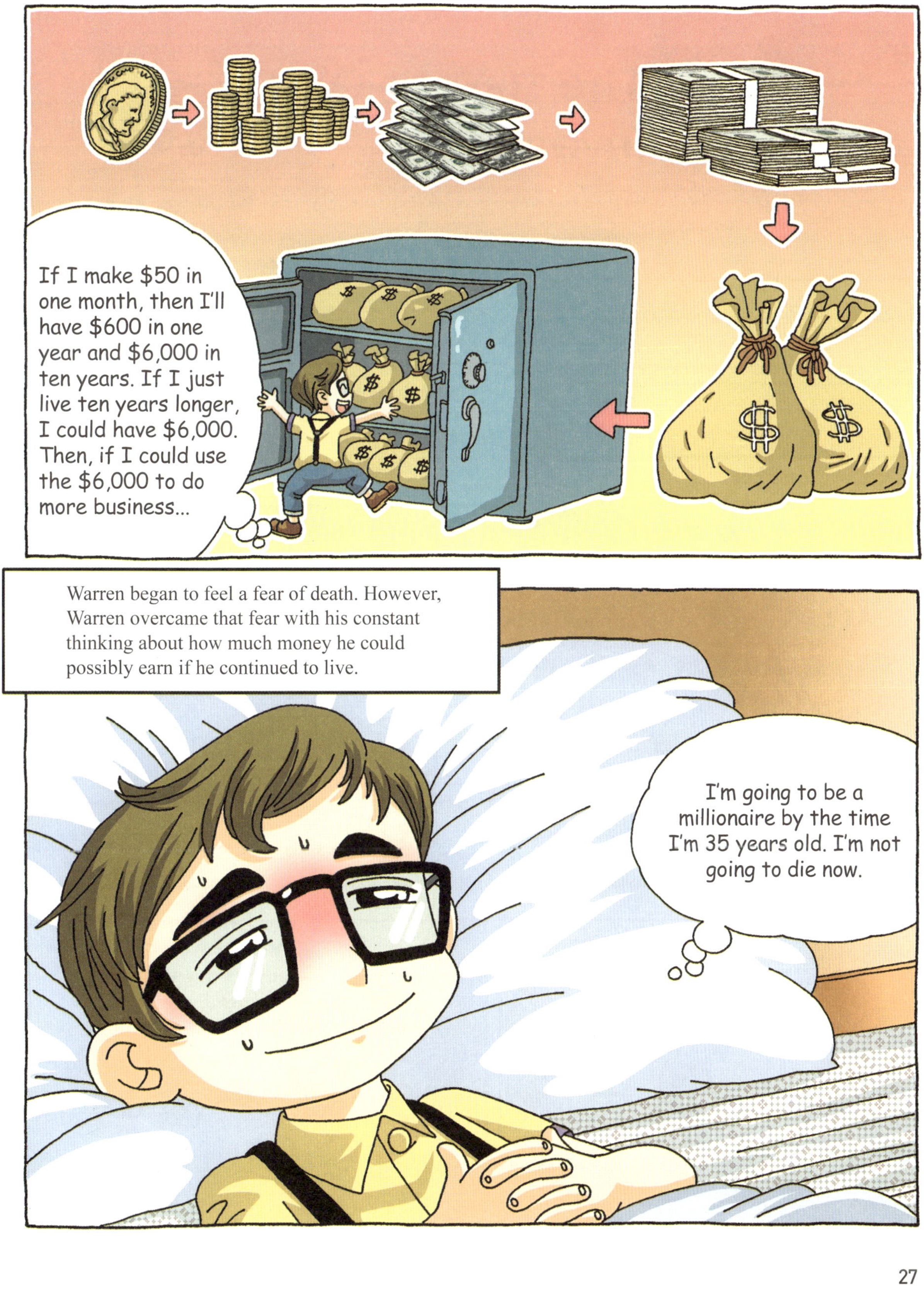

Warren began to feel a fear of death. However, Warren overcame that fear with his constant thinking about how much money he could possibly earn if he continued to live.

02
The 11-Year-Old Investor

Having recovered from his fever, Warren went out to continue doing business.
Come buy Coke! Coke!

However, when he thought about how he could die at any given moment, he did not feel satisfied with selling Coke. Warren and his friend Stu formulated a new business plan that would help them both earn money faster.
Do you want to do business with me?
Business? We're allowed to sell things, too?

There's a golf course right by our town. We'll sell the balls that we find. Since we'll be getting the golf balls for free, we'll make a ton of money.

Really? Then I'll be able to buy as many snacks as I want!
Of course.

In order to start their used golf ball business,
Warren and Stu began to find and gather golf balls.

Since their plans to sell used golf balls failed, Warren and Stu decided to sell popcorn and Coke at the football stadiums instead.

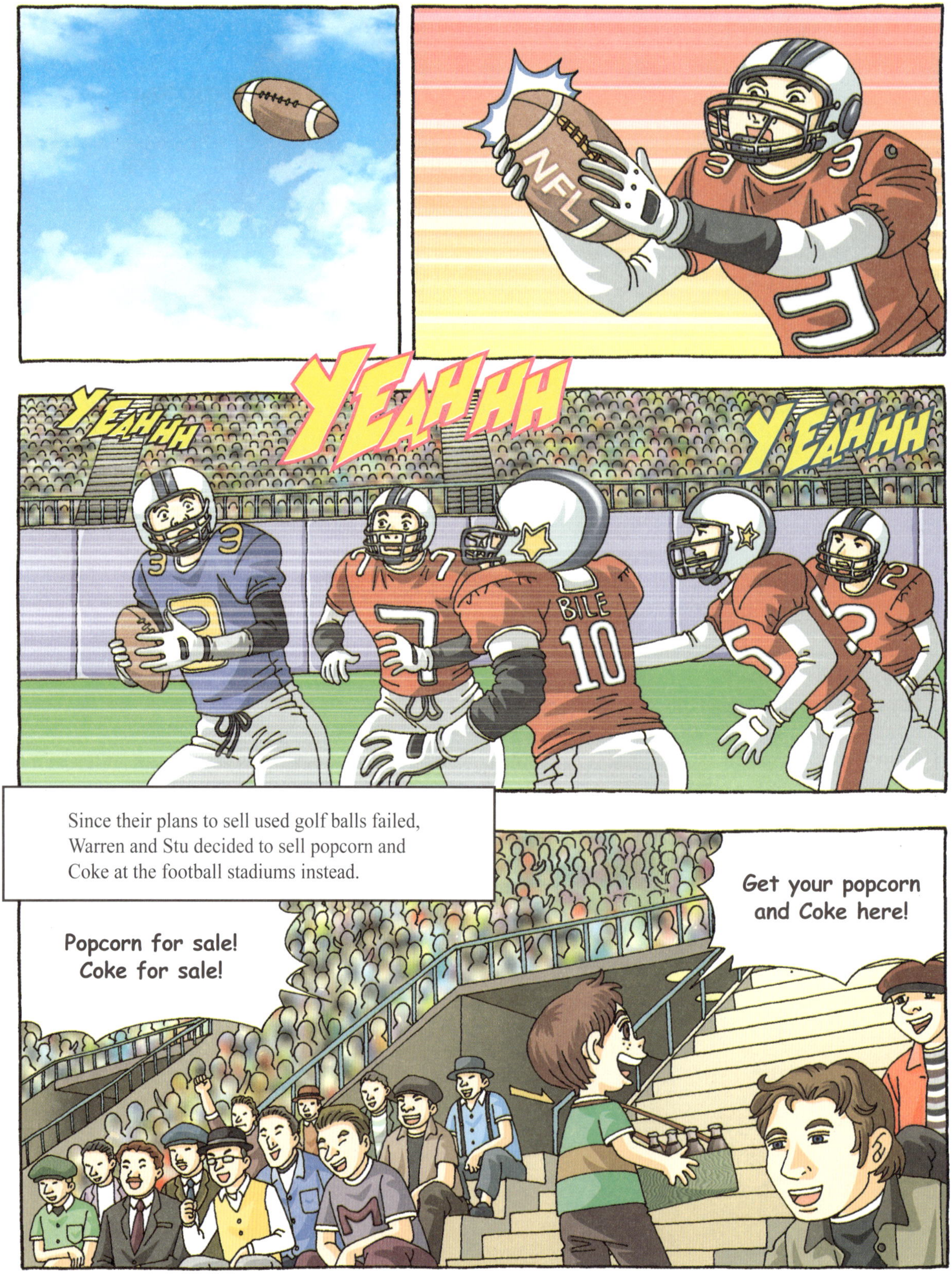

One day, Warren's father came home with an exceptionally bright look on his face.

Warren's father, Howard, was a stockbroker. His job was to buy and sell stocks, and he would earn money from commissions.
Yup, I earned a huge commission this time.

Dad, do people earn a lot of money from stocks?

No, it's not always like that. Of course making money is an additional benefit but it isn't the main purpose of trading stock. A little confusing, huh?
Tell me more about stocks, please.

Hmm... Warren, imagine this. You want to open up a business but you have no money. What do you do?
I'd have to borrow money.

Correct. You'd have to borrow money. But starting a business takes a lot of money so borrowing from just a couple people won't be enough. That's why you need to agree to issue shares.
Hey everyone, I just started a business. I will be selling shares, so please buy them.

If you continue to do business in that manner, you'd make some profit, right? The more profit your company makes, the more money your company has. Then, as a result, your company will continue to grow and it's value would increase.

If the value of your company increases, the price of the shares goes up as well. If the price of shares for Warren Company went up from $1 to $2, what would happen?

*capital: Money invested in the business for profit.

Correct. However, among the people who own shares of your company, there may be some that don't think they need them anymore and sell them.
You've heard of Warren Company, right? I own 100 shares of that company but I want to sell 10 of them.
Oh, the shares that used to be 1 dollar each? I'll buy them off of you.
You do know that the price of the hares rose to $2 because the company grew, right? That'll be $20.
Alright. Since this is a company with value, I'll buy the shares even if they're a little pricey.

Then this lady just made 1 dollar for each of the 10 shares, or in other words, she made a 10 dollar profit, you see? This buying and selling of stocks is called stock trading.
But Dad, do the prices of stocks ever fall?

Of course. If the company's value falls, so do their stocks. That's why you need to look carefully at the companies before you buy shares in them.

Oh!

Warren became interested in stock trades so he began to study and learn more about stocks. Thus, for Warren, his father's den was the best library because it contained a very large amount of books that had to do with stocks.

Warren, what are you doing in Dad's den?

Warren!
Ah, Doris!

Take a look at this.
Is it something funny?

Yeah, this is a new book on techniques and strategies for value investing.
The Intelligent Investor

When people are investing in stocks, they tend to buy a lot of shares when they see prices rising a bit, and they tend to sell their shares when they see prices falling.
The Intelligent

However, Benjamin Graham says that people should believe in the companies that they are invested in, and hold onto their shares.
What good will come of that?

Here it is! If you're invested for a long time, you will gain profit...
The p... p... profit...

The profit, what?
No one can measure the profit!
This means that through value investing, I could become a millionaire?
What? Millionaire? What kind of nonsense is that? What, you're just going to get all that money just because you hold onto your shares?
Ugh!

In order to practice what he had learned in the books, Warren went to the stock brokerage by where his dad worked, and carefully watched the movement of the stock prices.

Hey kid, what's so interesting?
Huh?

Your eyes are sparkling. I've never seen someone so concentrated on something before.

It's fun. Heh heh.

But what are you looking at?
I'm recording the flow of the stocks. If I look at this, I'll know that after the shares have risen, they must fall. Falling shares will eventually rise again, as well.

Then will you take a look at the shares I bought yesterday? The prices keep falling.
This company's shares have been declining for a few days now. In about 3 days, it should go back up.

Hahaha, really? I was actually going to sell these shares tonight but I guess I'll wait a few more days.

A few days later, Warren was, again, sitting in the stock brokerage building, carefully observing the conditions of the stock trades.

Warren became the young star of the stock brokerage. Many people would ask Warren about the prospects of their stocks, and Warren would answer them the best that he could.

Warren, why don't you try directly investing in some stocks now?
Me? Invest?

Warren tried to convince his sister, Doris, to invest in stocks with him.
I told you I don't want to do it.
Doris, you don't have to do anything and you'll be making money.

Still, I said no! Why are you trying to do whatever you want with my allowance?
But I won't be using any of it. You can buy your stock under your name.

Eventually, Warren convinced Doris to invest, and he bought 3 shares of Cities Service each for him and his sister. Each share was $37 which was a lot of money for the young siblings.

However, unlike Warren's prediction, the price of Cities Service shares started to drop. When Doris found out about this, she was angry at Warren.

Cities Service continued to drop. Warren could not hide his disappointment. The more time passed, the harsher Doris' words were.
...

I heard the shares dropped again today! When the hell are we ever going to make money?
Ahhh, I don't know!

Should we just sell the shares before any more damage is done? Ah, what should I do? Not only am I losing my money but it looks like I'm going to lose all of Doris' money, too!

Warren would visit the stock brokerage every day with an uneasy mind.

Yes, that's it!
CITIES SERVICE ↑ 5
It finally happened! Woo!
Oh, Dad!

I'm guessing that the stocks went up?
Yes, I want to sell them immediately.
Sell them? Hmm, that's your choice but don't regret it later on.
I won't. The $37 shares went up to $40 each, which means that we're making $3 per share. Doris and I made $9!
Warren sold the stock and gave his sister the proudly earned money.
Oh my gosh, we really did make money!
BANK BOOK
Happy now?
Warren, I have some bad news for you.

Cities Service shares increased every day and eventually one share was worth $202. Warren was shocked.

Warren, when it comes to investments, you need to have patience. If you trusted a company's value enough to invest in that company, than instead of becoming nervous because of the money, you should probably believe in the company and wait patiently.
Yes, and next time I should only recommend other people to invest when I'm absolutely positive about it.

Haha, you're still young. You still have an endless amount of opportunities ahead of you. However, try to engrave today's lesson into your mind.
Okay, Dad.

Haha, you fireball of a son!
Ah, Dad, that tickles!

03 A Young Entrepreneur

Track 20 ▶

When Warren was 13 years old, his family had to move to Washington D.C. because his father, Howard, had been elected for the House of Representatives.

Warren never really got along with his peers so it was difficult for him to adjust to his new life, and thus he spent a lot of time alone.

Hey, do you happen to know where the classroom for Science is located?
Huh?

My next class is Science but I don't know where to go.

Oh, I... have English in this room...

Oh really? Anyway, you don't know where the Science classroom is?
Y-yeah...

What were you talking to that geek about?

I was curious about what kind of kid he was but he couldn't even speak properly.

He doesn't look smart at all.
That's surprising. I thought he studied a lot.

Newspaper Agency
Hiring Delivery Man
Then one day, Warren discovered something as he walked past a newspaper store.
Ah, I'm so bored. School is boring and I can't do any business. If I want to become a millionaire, I can't be wasting time like this...

Hiring Delivery Man

Warren started working as the paper delivery boy. The newspapers that he was delivering were *The Washington Post*.

Track 22 ▶

When he was done delivering newspapers, he would go around to different houses and try to get new readers. The more readers, the more newspapers to deliver, and thus, the more money Warren would make.
305

I don't think the person in this place reads newspapers.
307

Is anybody home?
KNOCK
KNOCK

What do you want?
Hello.

Sir, are you interested in reading newspapers?

Newspapers?

Yes, you see, I deliver *The Washington Post* newspapers.
The Washington Post? I didn't think much of that newspaper.

A real newspaper is *The Washington Times-Herald*. That's the best.

Then I'll get that one for you. Would you like to receive newspapers?
Really? Sure, then.

Heh heh, thank you!

Unlike other delivery boys and girls, Warren wanted to increase the number of different kinds of newspapers that he would deliver.
I heard you're delivering The Washington Times-Herald, too, now?

Yeah, there are quite a few people who read that.
But won't it be tiring and time-consuming?

It's okay. I just need to be a little bit more diligent.

You're doing this because the more newspapers you sell the more you get paid, right?
You're right.

Psh, good luck with that!
You think the rest of us don't deliver more because we don't know we'll get paid more?
Well, time to start!

As the number of newspapers Warren had to deliver, grew, he found out ways to get things done faster and more efficiently. He would divide the area into sections based on the newspapers people wanted. He also noted which routes were the shortest between houses.

As a result, he would finish his work faster than the other deliverers.

Heh heh, I finished earlier than usual today.

I'm done with my deliveries, boss!

Why are you so late? I waited a long time for you.

Agency

Warren was not satisfied with just delivering papers in the morning. He decided to deliver the evening newspaper, the *Evening Star*, as well. Not only that but he also gradually expanded the delivery area.

CREAK
...

What's wrong with your expression? Did something bad happen to you?

Mr. Richard moved away without a word.
What? Mr. Richard was the one who extended his subscription by 3 months. He probably did it on purpose since he knew he was going to move away!

I'm subtracting Mr. Richard's subscription fees from your pay since you were responsible for collecting it from him!

Sigh...

You should be careful, too! There are so many bad people in the world!
Oh, okay. Yeah.

You rascal. Why are you taking your anger out on Warren?
Ouch!

KNOCK
KNOCK

Who is it?

On Monday night, Warren went to look for Mr. Billy.

Aren't you the paper delivery boy? What brings you here?

Hello, Mr. Billy. I've come to collect your newspaper subscription fee.

Isn't the subscription fee supposed to be paid once a month? I already paid it last week.
But you're moving away tomorrow so I need to collect your subscription money for up till the day you move.

What the.. how did you know I was going to move?
You will pay the subscription, right?

Of course! Do I look like someone who'd rip people off? Hahaha.

What's this?

It's all the money from people who have moved or people who were behind on paying for their subscriptions.
Wh-what?

Warren! You're such a great guy. I think I need to promote you. From now on, you'll have the 'Westchester' section.

Oh! That place is so big, it'll probably be hard for him to do it alone, boss.
This guy can do it. He found out all the people who were going to move away and collected subscription fees from all of them!

Seriously?

KNOCK
KNOCK

Warren, what are you up to?

*tax return: People with an income write down how much they're going to pay on a document before they pay their taxes.

I never thought about that. For now, I'm just going to keep saving up money until I become a millionaire. It's my dream to become a millionaire someday.

Warren, saving up money is important but spending money is just as important. Saving up would just be for your own satisfaction, but what value would the money have?

Ah, I never thought about that. So what should I do if I wanted to use the money in a valuable way?
Haha, that's something that you should take your time and think about. Afterall, it's your money.

What Dad said was right. I can't just keep saving up all this money and not do anything with it. However, I don't want to spend it on just anything. What would be good to spend money on?
Eh! I can just think of that later when I become a millionaire.

Yeah, you should do it when you want to. Alright, so can I take a look at your tax return form?

Yes, here you go.

Damn, Warren. You earn $175 a month? At your age, that's really impressive. There are adults who don't even earn this much.

Anyway, I am a little worried about you.
Huh?

There are a lot of things you need to do at your age. What you need right now is an education.
But I...

I'm not telling you to quit working as a paper delivery boy. I'm just telling you not to slack off in school and use your work as an excuse.

A few years later, Warren graduated from high school. At that point, Warren had $6,000. To reach that $6,000, Warren didn't spend a single penny of that money in 2 years and 4 months.

However, the happiest news for Warren, wasn't the money he had collected. The best thing for Warren was that he was able to keep the promise that he had made to his father.

04

Going to College

Warren, recently graduated from high school, and his father were experiencing a conflict.

That's just child's play. You'll change your mind once you go to college and start learning about things properly.

Warren, you should listen to your father. There are schools that have accepted you.

Then what about delivering newspapers? I want to be able to continue doing that while I attend college.
What on earth are you saying? You can't look at a college education as something that is trifling. You're obviously going to have to quit your newspaper delivery job.

Sigh...

Warren!
Okay.

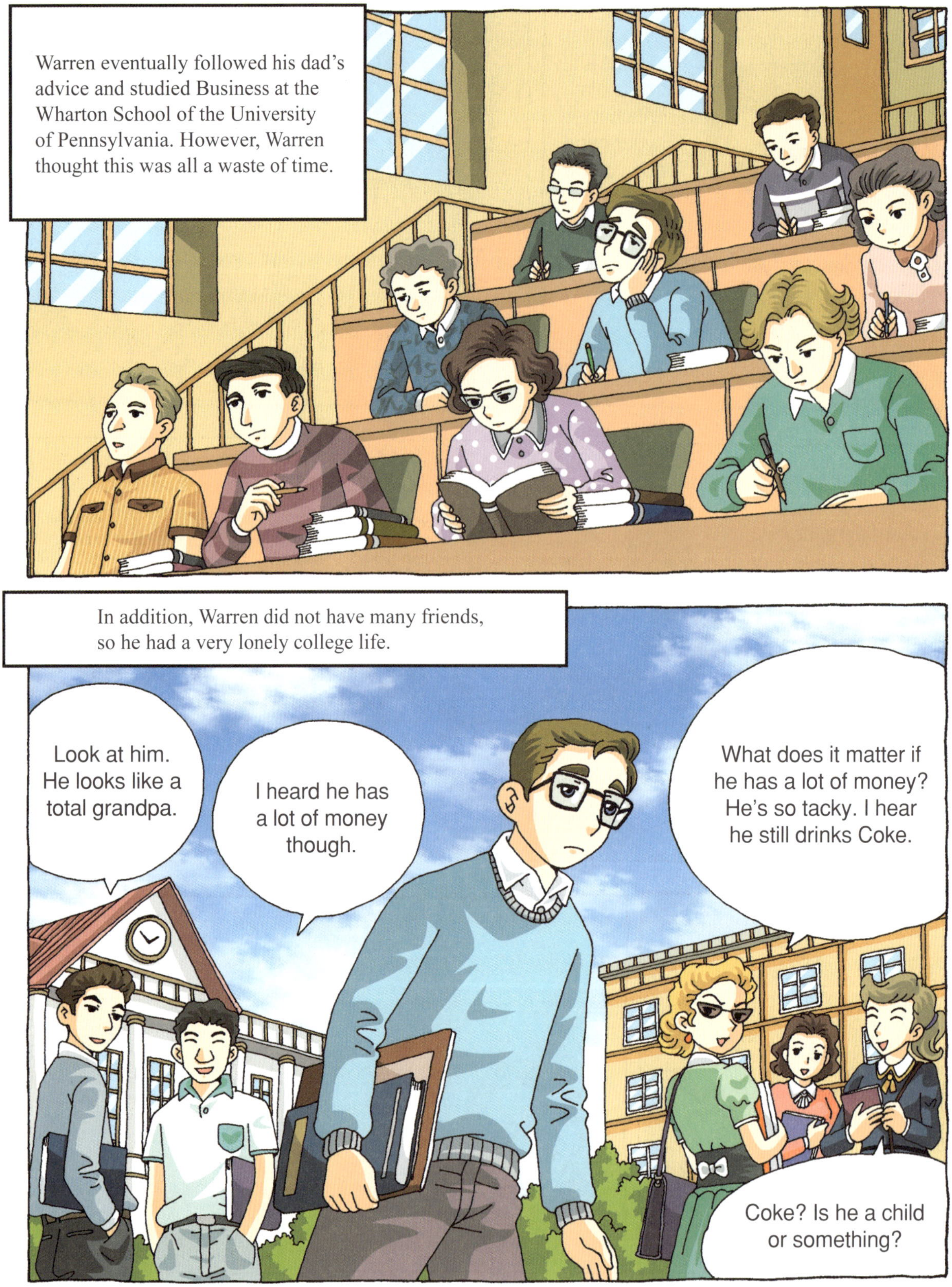

Warren eventually followed his dad's advice and studied Business at the Wharton School of the University of Pennsylvania. However, Warren thought this was all a waste of time.

In addition, Warren did not have many friends, so he had a very lonely college life.

Then one day, Warren's father, Howard Buffett, dropped out of the House of Representatives election after being in office for four terms.

CD Track 32 ▶

No, it's not that.
I would like to transfer
to the University of
Nebraska–Lincoln for
the remainder of my
college career.
Please, let me do it
my way this time.

Warren transferred to the University of
Nebraska-Lincoln, which was located
close to his hometown. He also started
to manage the newspaper delivery boys.
Listen up, because I'm about
to teach you a strategy
that will help you collect
subscription payments
from people who are
about to move away.

Of course he did not
neglect his stock
investments, either.

In 1950, Warren graduated from college one year faster than others in his class. During that time, Warren's personal wealth had grown to $9800.
Click

Warren, what are you going to do now?
Since you graduated from college, I won't stop you if you say you want to start your own business.

No. After going to college, I think that it would be a good idea for me to study some more. I'm going to apply for graduate school.

That's great news. Which graduate school are you thinking about applying to?

Harvard, the best school in America.

Harvard?

In order to get into the Harvard Business School, Warren went to do an interview.

TAS
...

Mr. Buffett?

Yes.
What did you bring with you?
It-it's a chart about stocks. It's a field that I am very confident about, so I wanted to speak about it.

You may begin.
Uh...
HARVARD

Oops?

TAS
HARVARD

A-as you can see...
shares have a
constant flow...

Mr. Buffett.
H-h-here, if you take a look at Kaiser-Frazer's stock trading...
VE RI TAS
HAVARD
Mr. Buffett!
Yes?

I don't think you have what we are looking for in a student. Why don't you come back in a few years?

Warren was rejected during his Harvard Business School interview. For the first time in his life, Warren, who had succeeded in everything he had ever tried to do, knew how it felt to fail.

You guys are making a huge mistake. I'm a really talented person!
Harvard? We'll see. They're all going to regret having rejected me!
Warren returned home, dejected. Warren's father tried to comfort him.
Don't worry too much, Warren. There are still so many schools you can choose from.
For example, Columbia may not be as good as Harvard, but it's still recognized as one of the most prestigious schools on the East Coast.
...

Sigh, I'm not interested. I don't even know what schools are good...

Aha!

However, Benjamin Graham says that people should believe in the companies that they are invested in, and hold onto their shares.
Benjamin Graham's book did say that we'd have to wait a long time...
Columbia University
Benjamin Graham

You know what, Dad? I think I will apply to Columbia for graduate school.
See? Didn't I tell you you'd find a school that you'd want to attend?

But Warren, I don't think Columbia is an option.

Huh? Why?

There isn't much time left until the application deadline. Even if you were to send in the application today, I think they would receive it past the deadline date.

...

But Father, I want to learn from Professor Benjamin Graham. It might not make it on time, but I still want to send in an application.

Warren really put his heart and soul into writing his application. He wrote about how he had earned money working as a newspaper delivery boy, and how much profit he had made from investing in stocks. He also wrote about his thoughts on stock investments and management.

Warren wanted to learn about business from Benjamin Graham, who he was familiar with from his childhood readings. However, Warren's application was received past the deadline.
Benjamin Graham

The professors of Columbia's Business School had a debate over Warren's application.
After reading this young man's application, I can see that he is very gifted. What do you think about accepting him into our school?

But, his application was handed in late as it was received past the due date. It is important to meet with deadlines.

I agree. He does show a lot of talent and promise, but the fact that his application did not meet the deadline is troubling.

...

A few days later, Warren received a letter in the mail.
Warren, you have mail from Columbia University.

Do you think it's my acceptance letter?
Go ahead and read it.

We have reviewed your application for admission to our school; however, your application was received after the deadline. Thus, the University has come to the conclusion that you should not be eligible for admission...

I got rejected again.
Warren, just like you have to have patience when investing in stocks, you also should not jump to conclusions in other areas of life. Read the letter all the way to the end.

Sigh.

but by the end of the meeting...
we were partial to your gifted talents and so we'd like to notify you of your acceptance...

...into our school.

It's an acceptance letter, Dad!
Would you look at that! I told you not to jump to conclusions.

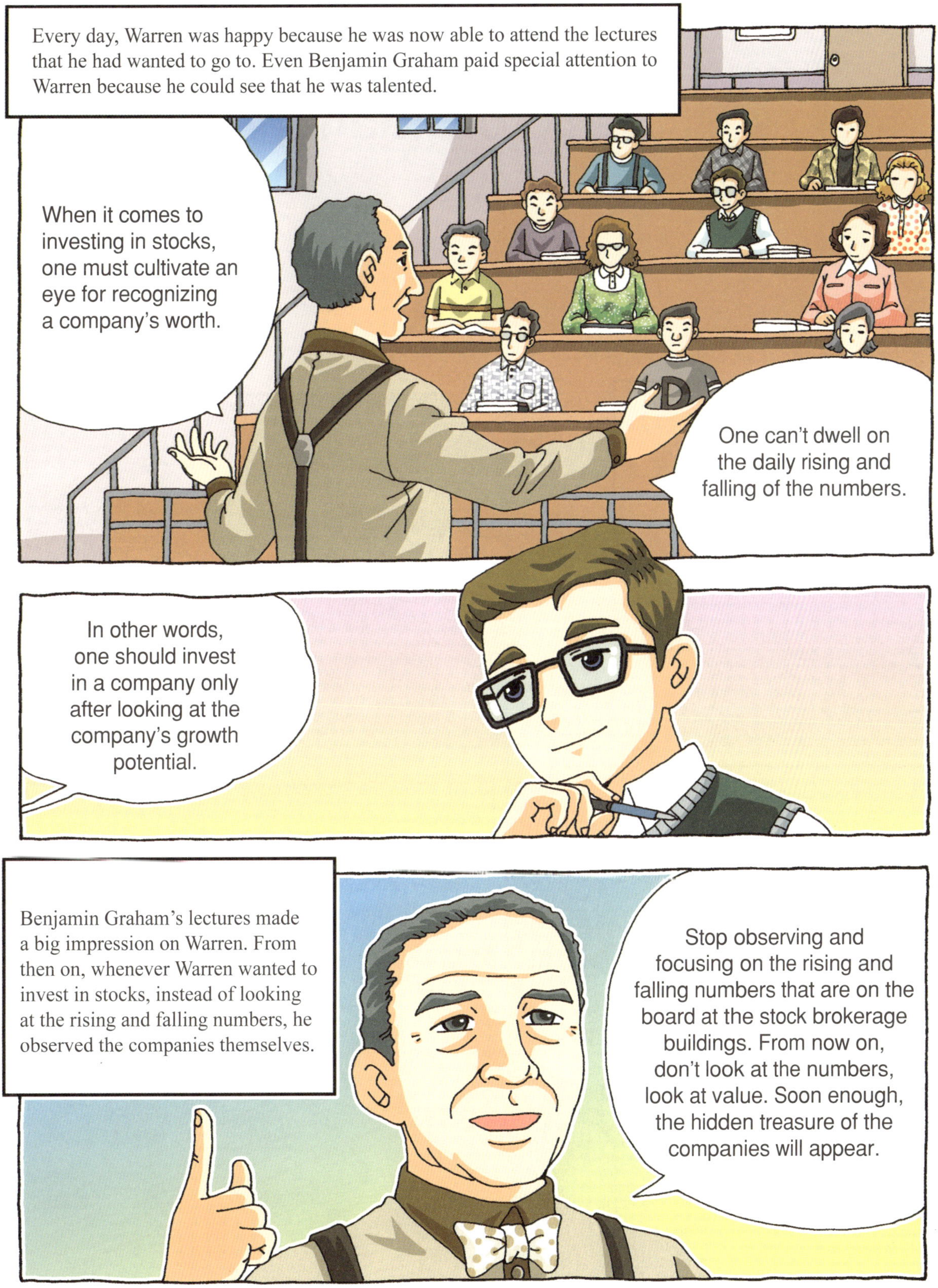

Every day, Warren was happy because he was now able to attend the lectures that he had wanted to go to. Even Benjamin Graham paid special attention to Warren because he could see that he was talented.

Benjamin Graham's lectures made a big impression on Warren. From then on, whenever Warren wanted to invest in stocks, instead of looking at the rising and falling numbers, he observed the companies themselves.

05

Back to Omaha

Warren returned to Omaha to work for his father's stock brokerage firm, Buffett-Falk & Co.

Okay, that's all for now.
I will stop by again later.

People who had consultations with Warren were very likely to rise and leave by the end of it. With the exception of a few people, everyone who spoke to Warren would not invest in the companies that he had recommended.
...

Haha, after speaking with you, I feel certain. Sure enough, it was good that I did not take the other guy's advice.

Are you talking about Warren? That guy is always trying to recommend people to invest in companies that are not very well known and pretty much unheard of.

Tsk, tsk. I guess he's not very talented. But then again, what do we expect from such a young man?

HOWARD
Did you summon me?

Warren, rumor has it that you don't have many clients. I was wondering if you were experiencing any problems.
There's no problem, really.
HOWARD

I heard that one of the companies you're investing in is a news agency?
Yes. As of right now, this company doesn't get much attention but it's going to become a very great and valuable company in the future.

And how far in the future is this, exactly?
Probably about a year or two from now?
HOWARD

To clients, waiting one or two years is a lot to ask for. Of course it's best to be patient when investing in stocks but...

...clients won't want that. Instead of coming to you for advice, they'll go to someone else. Then, you'll be out of work.
That's why I'm saying this but why don't you try compromising with clients at a proper level.

Compromise?
Introduce them to stocks that will pay off immediately in front of their eyes.
HOW

Dad, I still have clients who come to me for advice, even though I know that there aren't that many of them. If I switch my approach to investments in order to gain more new clients, it would seem rude to the few loyal clients that I have right now.

Although people worried for Warren, Warren did not compromise his approach for investments and he continued to do things his way. Now two years have passed by.

Hey, do you remember me?

Oh, yes, I do.

Remember that company you kept recommending that I invest in? What was it... the news agency.
Yes.

After two years, Warren had become very popular at the stock brokerage firm. This was because the price of stocks in every company that Warren picked, would increase sharply.

Noticing Warren's outstanding abilities, his alma mater, the University of Nebraska-Lincoln asked him to give a lecture about investments. This lecture would be part of the community education program that the University had. Warren gladly accepted.

Because the community education program was open to local residents and to the general public, the ages of the attendants ranged greatly. The average age of the people there was around the late 40s.

Hello, I'm Warren Buffett and I will be giving lectures here for one semester.

Isn't he a little too young?

stock
We will begin our first class now.
What is stock? As you all may know...

I think that lecturer is my son's friend.
stock
Exactly my point. What on earth are we supposed to learn from someone so young?

Warren worked hard on his lectures but the students did not take him seriously because he was so young. Day by day, the number of students attending his lectures would decrease. There was even a day when only four students showed up to his lecture.

Sigh, I guess my lectures don't seem very valuable to everyone.

But, a promise is a promise. If anything, I would like to keep my end of the deal for you guys. Today's topic will be 'Which Companies Should We Invest In?'

During this lecture, many people may be confused by the things they hear about the companies. This is mostly due to the fact that many people invest after only looking at the price of the shares.

However, the truth is, you must look at the company first before you invest in its shares. If you invest in a company that has a huge potential for growth...

...it will be hard to see that growth immediately, but in the near future there will be a huge payoff. A good company is one that continues to grow because then the value of its shares will grow, too.

When investing, you must look far off into the future. It is something that must be done with great patience. This is Value Investing.

You need patience in order to invest. You need to believe in your decisions and wait patiently.

Warren's lectures began to gradually gain peoples' recognitions.
Hey John, why don't you come out to the lectures?

Lectures? You mean the ones taught by that young kid?

He may be young but he's incredibly talented. Last night, he told us about Value Investing and it was awesome.

And that's not all! Apparently every share that he invested in is said to be hitting an all time high! He's very well known at the stock brokerage firm.

Seriously?

Sigh, I wonder how many people showed up today.
CLICK
Woah.

The more time passed, the more Warren became known as a very skilled lecturer. By the time the lectures were coming to an end, the lecture hall would be packed full with people and Warren was able to end his lectures successfully.

06 Workaholic

Although Warren Buffett would occasionally suffer from small failures, for the majority of the time he would be triumphantly successful in all his investments. By the time he was 26 years old, he was married and had a personal wealth of $150,000.

26-year-old Warren put his own family's name on the line and created the Buffett Partnership, Ltd. This is a gathering for the people who will all join an investment partnership so that they can all split the big payoff in the future. This investment partnership meeting consisted of 6 of Warren's friends, one of whom was his sister, Doris.

Buffett Partnership, Ltd.
First of all, I'd like to thank the six people who are here to take part in my investment partnership.
If you trust me with your investments, I will guarantee at least a 4% annual revenue rate.

Warren, so you're basically asking us to trust you to do anything you want with our money.
You're right, Doris. You guys won't be able to interfere with the investments I make. In return, no matter what, I will make sure to split the profit with you guys.

Well, I'm your sister so I trust you.
Warren, we're all friends here. Of course we trust you.

The revenue that Buffet Partnership, Ltd. yielded was amazing. The first year, they started off with a 10% profit but within 5 years, it had gone up to a whopping 251%. Sooner or later, the 7 member partnership had grown to consist of 90 members.

What is it, honey?

Susan, Buffett Partnership, Ltd. has $7.2 million now! Can you guess how much of that money is mine?
I-I'm not sure.

One million dollars! A million!

A m-million dollars?

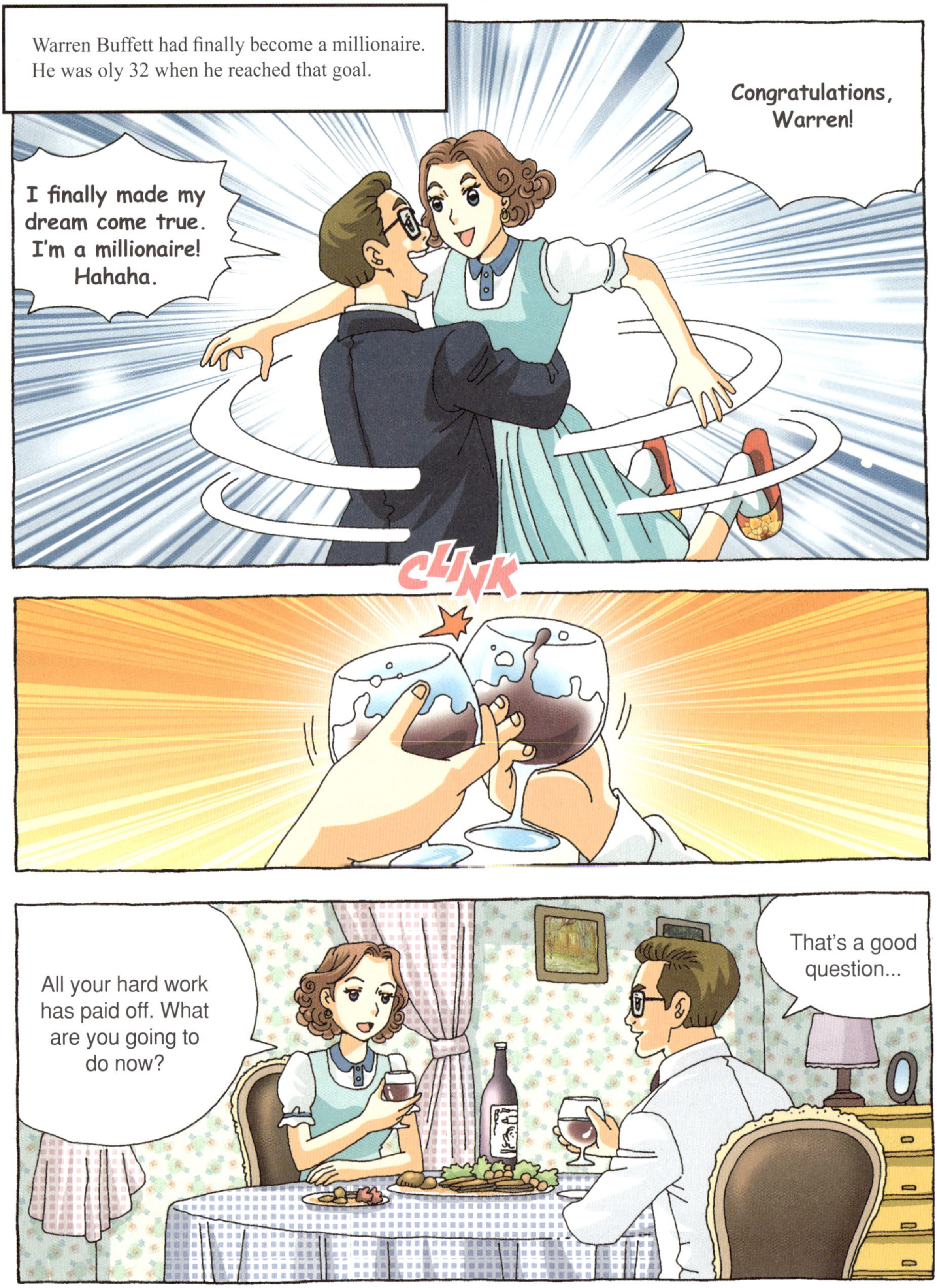

Warren Buffett had finally become a millionaire. He was oly 32 when he reached that goal.
Congratulations, Warren!
I finally made my dream come true. I'm a millionaire! Hahaha.
CLINK
All your hard work has paid off. What are you going to do now?
That's a good question...

Honestly, I think I reached my dream of becoming a millionaire too quickly. I didn't really plan anything beyond that.

Since you're so good at saving money, why don't you make becoming a billionaire your next goal?

Haha, that's too simple. Rather, I think I'll study the secret to fortune.
If I can figure out the secret to fortune and wealth, I'll be able to become the richest man in the whole world.

Warren was running on the Road to Success without failure. Then one day...
What? Are you serious?

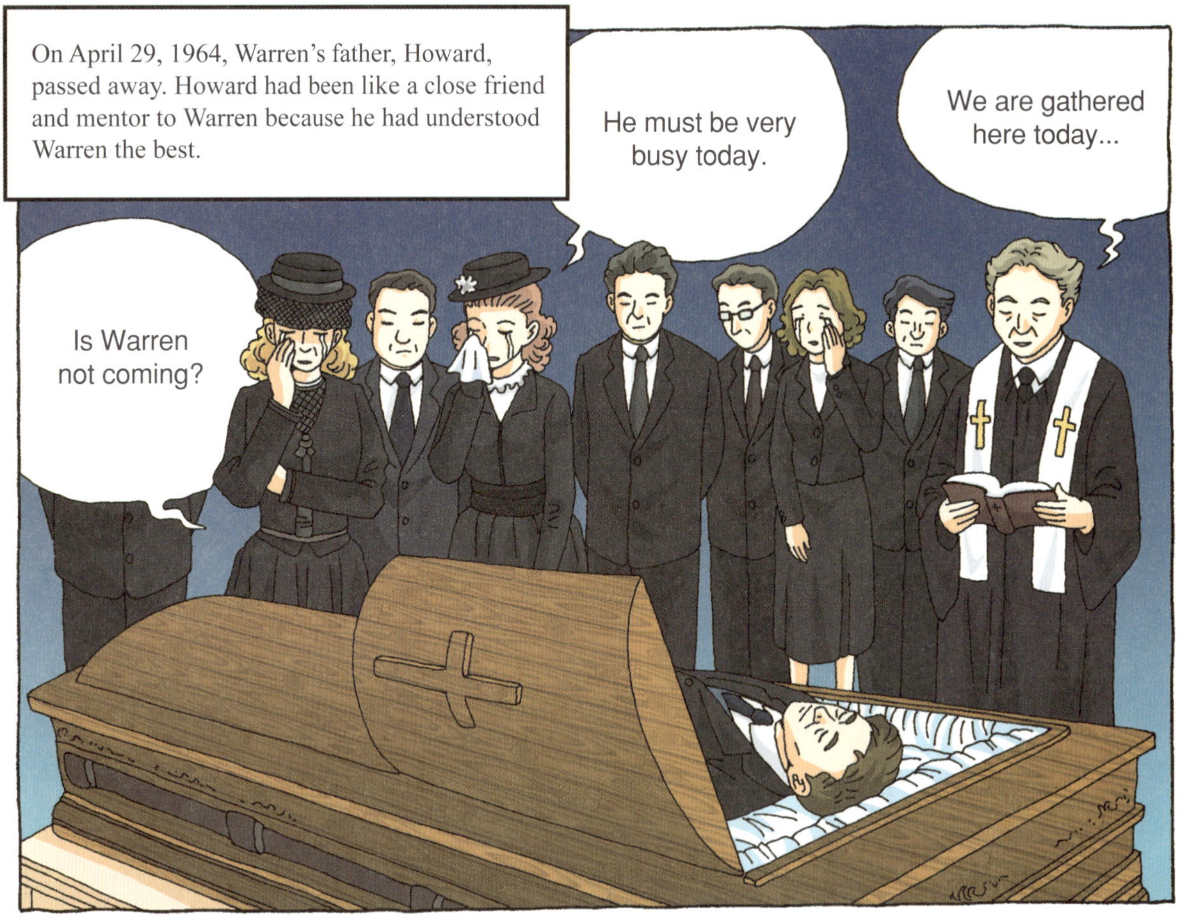

On April 29, 1964, Warren's father, Howard, passed away. Howard had been like a close friend and mentor to Warren because he had understood Warren the best.

Father!
Father!

Ahh!

I'm here, Dad.
Open your
eyes.
Warren, it's time
to let go.

Hold on.
Wait...

Warren had followed and loved his father very, very much. His father's death caused great grief for him.

In order to remember his father forever, Warren hung a portrait of his father in his office.

Warren, how are you feeling? How are the investments?

Sigh, I'm thinking about it. Doris, would there be any point in investing right now?
Warren Buffett

What are you talking about? These days the price of shares keeps increasing. If you don't invest now, then when would you?

Prices have never gone up so drastically before. Something is definitely wrong.
Isn't it good if the shares go up?

No, these shares are increasing abnormally. In situations like this, it's hard to tell which companies are worth investing in.

I'm not even sure if I should hold onto the shares that I already have anymore.
Well, either way, you can't just sit here and do nothing.

What about all the members of the investment partnership that have entrusted their money in you?

I already felt a heavy burden on my shoulders because I knew that all the members of the partnership would expect a lot from me. I thought about it, and I think this is my chance.
Chance for what?
Warren Buffett

I'm going to sell all the shares that I own. Also, I'm going to liquidate Buffett Partnership, Ltd.

What?

Warren, what's this we hear about you shutting down Buffett Partnership, Inc.?
The Partnership is making so much Revenue. Why do you suddenly want to shut it down?

I'm thinking about going in another direction with investments.

And what's that?
Let us in on it.

Right now, in this market, it's hard to tell which companies are really worth investing in.
In abnormal markets like this, even companies that have value will get bad assessments.

I'm going to find those companies. Then I'm going to save the companies by making sure that they get correct assessments.

The correct businesses?

I don't know. Just buy some shares from Berkshire Hathaway. My investment will be made through that company.
Berkshire Hathaway? Isn't that a failing textile company?

You're right. It's a company that no one cares about. That's why I chose it.

What are you trying to say? Can you explain it more simply?

Buffet Partnership, Ltd. became too well known. It's to the point where other partnerships are going to try to copy Buffet Partnership, Ltd.

If we go in the same direction that everyone else is investing in, we'll yield less revenue. For me, that is a huge burden because I am responsible for the revenues of all the members of our partnership.
...

That's why I'm going to save Berkshire Hathaway and use it so that my presence will go undetected.

After that day, Warren began to look for new places to invest in.
There has to be a great company out there that contributes to society and follows correct business ethics, but is not fully appreciated for its true value and worth.

Ah, this is the place!

GEICO INSURANCE

I'm here to sign up for insurance. Where can I get a consultation?
안 내

I'm sorry, sir. We would love for you to get insurance but I must inform you that our company's assessments are bad right now. Would you still be interested?

The company's assessment is bad? The General Manager must be a lousy person.
No, that's not the case. The General Manager is a wonderful person who works day and night trying to save the company.

Then the company shouldn't have gotten to this point, no?

Warren invested $4,000,000 into Geico Insurance Company. Geico became financially stable and the people who had hesitated to sign up for Geico before, came back to sign up for Geico Insurance. Warren was able to save Geico, a company that had been on the verge of bankruptcy.

One day, while looking for a new company to invest in, Warren stumbled upon a small furniture company in Omaha. In order to check if his information was correct, Warren went to visit the store's founder.

Now I might just be watching over the store but up till recently, I was operating the company.

Oh, so you founded this company!

Correct. I stopped operating the whole business but my son still works day and night, making cheap, good quality furniture.
From a customer's point of view, that sounds wonderful, but if you sell good quality furniture for cheap, don't you make very little profit?

Truthfully, the business isn't doing so well these days. The business is in such a shaky situation that it wouldn't be a surprise if it went bankrupt tomorrow.

Oh, no. The thought of this company closing down after 55 years has got me all teary-eyed. I'm so sorry.

There's still hope. Don't be so disappointed.
Of course. Here, take a look around.

I'll come back. I have to buy a lot of furniture so I think I should make a shopping list first.

Warren!
SLAM

Oh, it's you.
Is it true that you're about to invest in some weird little furniture store?

Are you talking about Nebraska Furniture Mart? I was going to talk about it at the shareholders' meeting tomorrow.

How much are you investing?

$60 million.

What? $60 million? Why are you putting so much money into such a tiny store?
This is probably the most I've ever invested in one company.

I can't let you do this! Not this time. Everyone's worried.
That store passed my test. I'm certain about this.

Your test? And what would that be?
Rather than looking at the immediate performance results of the company, I look at the spirit of the company.
Nebraska Furniture Mart's General Manager doesn't operate the store just for the money.

Yeah, right. There's no such thing as a company that doesn't work for the money.

It's right here. The Blumkin family considers it more important to provide cheap, good quality furniture for its customers than to make money. As a result, the store's revenue continued to decrease.

This company is exactly what I was looking for. It operates based on correct business ethics. And plus, I am not only investing in companies.
Then? Where else did you invest?

I'm investing in General Managers who have the right spirit. These Managers will definitely lead their company's in the right direction.

So don't worry.

Warren invested $60 million into the unknown furniture company. Even though this was a lot of money, Warren thought it was worth every penny. With the repetition of these things, Warren became known as the "Sage of Omaha."

Truly Rich

Track 57 ▶

Warren continued to invest in stocks and he gained enormous wealth. He is also consistently ranked in the forefront of the world's richest people.

It never occurred to me that one of the top five richest people in the world would work in such a humble building.
And you're even having a hamburger and Coke as your meal.

Haha, just because one has a lot of money doesn't mean that one must work in a huge office and eat expensive food.

That's true but when people become rich they usually want to live a lavish lifestyle.

Hahaha, is that so? Well, anyway, is there a particular reason why you came to see me?
Yes. I came to deliver this to you. It's an invitation to a party Bill Gates and his family are having.

Hmm, a party?
He'd really appreciate it if you came.

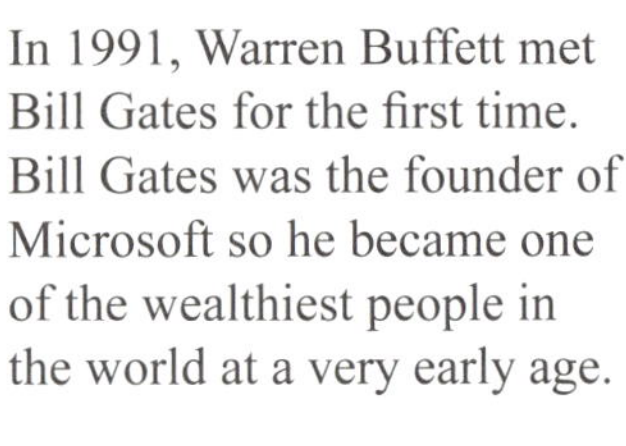

In 1991, Warren Buffett met Bill Gates for the first time. Bill Gates was the founder of Microsoft so he became one of the wealthiest people in the world at a very early age.

Drinking Coke at a party? That person must be unfamiliar with places like this.
What? You don't know who that is?

Hello, Mr. Warren Buffett?
W-Warren Buffett?

It's so nice to meet you, Mr. Bill Gates.
Hello, and you too.

I'm guessing you like to drink Coke?
I like hamburgers, too.

Haha, this is surprising. I never thought that the richest man in the world would like to drink Coke and eat burgers.

This is good enough for me. Anyway, I've always really wanted to get a chance to meet you, Mr. Gates.
Me?

Yes. The people around me are all so old, I thought it would be nice to make a young friend.
Hahaha, I'd gladly be your friend.

Even though Warren and Bill were 25 years apart in age, they still got along very well and became very close friends. Bill gates even produced books such as *The Road Ahead* for people like Warren, who don't know much about computers.

The Gates couple and Warren got along very well. They would go watch performances together and even dine together.

What did you think of tonight's performance?
It was fun. Very fun, haha.

Since you two treated me to an enjoyable performance, I'll buy you both dinner in return.
This place will be more expensive than a Coke and hamburger.
Food
Restaur

Hahaha! Eat as much as you want. This is nothing. I can do at least this much for someone who changed my life.

What do you mean, changed your life?
The both of you have introduced me to a whole new world. Before I met you two, I was just a nincompoop who just kept saving up money.
I didn't know how to spend my money properly, and I just enjoyed watching the numbers grow so much that I just kept clutching onto my savings.
You must've really enjoyed tonight's performance.
Yup, now I want to enjoy my life properly!

Then one day, a very shocking incident occurred.

What?

Bill Gates, 2 years after his declaration to do charitable work!
Still hundreds of millions of children
of hunger

Ah!

Warren was impressed by Bill Gates' charitable activities so he went to the Bill and Melinda Gates Foundation, which was operated by the couple.

That is true. In order to operate with a lot of money, the organization would have to be big, too. What kind of charity work do you do at this foundation?

At first, we were doing things in support of medical treatment and education for the poor in America. Nowadays, we help starving children in Africa.

Africa?

Yes. In the past, there was a time when Bill and I had gone to Africa. When we arrived, we were incredibly shocked. We saw so many children who were starving to death because they didn't have anything to eat.

This changed our lives. Bill wants to strive to set up a charity soon.

Would it be extreme to use the money from the foundation to start the charity?

Haha, people think that because we're extremely rich, we'll never have problems operating the foundation. However, there are so many places that need a helping hand and we always feel the the lack of operating expenses.
It's a great idea. But wouldn't you think it's a waste if you spend all the money that you spent your whole life earning on a charity?
No.
Saving up money is for one's own satisfaction but it isn't eaningful. What's more important is how one uses that money.
Wait, but why do you ask? Are you...
No, it's nothing. I'll come visit again, next time.

Warren, saving up money is important but spending money is just as important. Saving up would just be for your own satisfaction, but what value would the money have?
...

RIIING

Mr. Warren, do you want to meet up sometime next week?

No, there's no need. I have something to tell you today.
As you know I've always been collecting money. Maybe I'm lucky but I don't even remember ever experiencing any huge failures.
I went from being a kid selling gum and Coke to one of the world's richest people.
But now I've come to realize something. A true rich person isn't defined by the amount of money he or she has. A true rich person is someone who is able to take the money they have, and share it with the world without asking for anything in return.
Money that only ever stays in the pocket of one person, is wasted. Since this money has been earned from society, it should also be given back to society.

I don't know what you're getting at...
Bill, you're operating your charitable foundation, right? The Bill and Miranda Gates Foundation.

I'd like to donate a portion of my wealth to your foundation.

Really? Thank you so much. Will you tell me how much you're planning on donating? I need to think up a business plan.
I'm ashamed to say it isn't very much. It'll be about $37 billion.

Wh-what?

Mr. Warren, I-I think you told me the wrong amount... how much did you say?

$37 billion is an enormous amount of money.
$37 billion. I'll be giving $37 billion.

A-are you sure? You're going to donate all that money all at once...
Hahaha, I'm embarassed.
Then does this mean that you're going to stop dealing with stocks?

No, I enjoy investing in stocks so I won't be stopping. However, I do need to find other pleasures for my life!

Other pleasures?

Warren did as he said he would. He left the desk, that he had spent so much of his life sitting in front of, to go out and enjoy life.

He also discovered that he had another talent, which was acting. He acted in a play called "Annie."

He also acted as the voice of the main character in the children's economic educational animation show, *Secret Millionaires Club*.

According to *Forbes* magazine, in 2008, Warren Buffett was the richest man in the world. He was worth $62 billion.

However, the reason why so many people respected Warren Buffett, was not because he had so much money. It's because rather than investing simply to earn more money, he invested to give back to society.

Warren's interest in making donations has had a big impact on his children, as well. His sons, Howard and Peter, and his daughter, Susan, all operate charitable organizations.

Warren Buffett is living the rest of his life in Omaha, his peaceful hometown. He was a rich person who knew how to share his wealth, and he always lived a humble and economical life. Many people love and adore Warren Buffett and refer to him as the "Sage of Omaha."

Word Search

● Find the words which are hidden horizontally, vertically and diagonally.

| entrepreneur | declaration | cultivate | interfere |
| entrust | consultation | founder | forefront |

Vocabulary

● Match each word to the correct meaning.

1. investor	• 겸손한
2. merchant	• 알뜰한
3. modest	• 투자자
4. donate	• 증권 중개인
5. economical	• 상인
6. foundation	• 재단
7. stockbroker	• 기부하다
8. repetition	• 평가
9. assessment	• 파산
10. insurance	• 반복
11. bankruptcy	• 이윤
12. profit	• 보험

3 Guess What?

● Guess what he said in the blank.

U.S. Money (1)

Coins

• penny $0.01

Head (Obverse : 앞면)　　　　　　　Tail (Reverse: 뒷면)

Abraham Lincoln　　　Lincoln Memorial(1959-2008)　Union shield(2010-present)

• nickel $0.05

Head　　　　Tail　　　　Head　　　　Tail

Thomas Jefferson　　Monticello　　Thomas Jefferson　　Monticello
(1938-2003)　　(1938-2003)　　(2006-present)　　(2006-present)

• dime $0.10

Head　　　　　　　　　　　　Tail

 Franklin D. Roosevelt
(1946-present)

 Torch with an olive branch and
an oak branch(1946-present)

• quarter $0.25

Head

 George Washington
(1999-present)

Tail

 Bald Eagle
(1965-1998)

Tail　　　　　　Tail　　　　　　Tail

State Quarter Series　　D.C. and U.S. Territories　America the Beautiful Quarters
(1990-2008)　　　　(2009)　　　　(2010-2021)

U.S. Money (2)

Bills

Obverse (앞면)	Reverse (뒷면)

• $1

George Washington

The Great Seal of the United

• $2

Thomas Jefferson

The Declaration of Independence

• $5

Abraham Lincoln

The Lincoln Memorial

<table>
<tr><th></th><th></th></tr>
</table>

● $10

Alexander Hamilton

The U.S. Treasury

● $20

Andrew Jackson

The White House

● $50

Ulysses S. Grant

The U.S. Capitol

● $100

Benjamin Franklin

The Independence Hall

1930년		미국 네브래스카 주 오마하에서 태어났습니다.
1936년	6세	콜라를 파는 사업을 시작했습니다.
1938년	8세	주식에 관심을 갖고 공부하기 시작합니다.
1941년	11세	처음으로 주식 투자를 하여 주당 3달러의 이익을 남깁니다.
1944년	14세	신문 배달로 벌어들인 수입으로 세금을 내기 시작했습니다.
1947년	17세	와튼스쿨에 입학합니다.
1949년	19세	네브래스카 대학으로 편입합니다.
1950년	20세	하버드 경영대학원 진학에 실패하고 컬럼비아 경영대학원에 진학하여 어릴 적부터 존경하는 인물이었던 벤자민 그레이엄의 제자가 되었습니다.
1951년	21세	컬럼비아 경영대학원을 졸업하여 본격적인 투자를 시작합니다. 네브래스카 대학에서 자신보다 나이가 많은 학생들을 가르칩니다.

1956년 26세 오마하에서 가족과 친구 7명을 모아 '버핏 투자 조합'을 만듭니다.

1962년 32세 버핏 투자 조합의 자산이 불어나 720만 달러가 되었는데
             이 중 102만 달러가 워렌의 몫이 되어 백만장자가 됩니다.

1965년 35세 버크셔 해서웨이의 주식을 주당 19달러에 사서 경영권을 얻습니다.

1969년 39세 버핏 투자 조합을 해체합니다.

1973년 43세 워싱턴포스트 신문의 주식을 사들여 경영권을 얻습니다.

1988년 58세 코카콜라의 주식을 매입해 7%의 지분을 갖게 됩니다.

2006년 76세 재산 520억 달러 중 370억 달러를 자선 단체에 기부하겠다고 밝힙니다.

2008년 79세 총 재산 620억 달러로 경제지 포브스가 선정한 세계 최고의 부자가 됩니다.

~현재   주식 투자, 자선 사업 참여, 취미 생활 등으로 노년을 보내고 있으며
             자신의 투자 사업을 계승할 후계자를 찾고 있습니다.

who? 01	Barack Obama	979-11-5639-023-7
who? 02	Charles Darwin	979-11-5639-024-4
who? 03	Bill Gates	979-11-5639-025-1
who? 04	Hillary Clinton	979-11-5639-026-8
who? 05	Stephen Hawking	979-11-5639-027-5
who? 06	Oprah Winfrey	979-11-5639-028-2
who? 07	Steven Spielberg	979-11-5639-029-9
who? 08	Thomas Edison	979-11-5639-030-5
who? 09	Abraham Lincoln	979-11-5639-031-2
who? 10	Martin Luther King, Jr.	979-11-5639-032-9
who? 11	Louis Braille	979-11-5639-033-6
who? 12	Albert Einstein	979-11-5639-034-3
who? 13	Jane Goodall	979-11-5639-035-0
who? 14	Walt Disney	979-11-5639-036-7
who? 15	Winston Churchill	979-11-5639-037-4
who? 16	Warren Buffett	979-11-5639-008-4
who? 17	Nelson Mandela	979-11-5639-009-1
who? 18	Steve Jobs	979-11-5639-010-7
who? 19	J. K. Rowling	979-11-5639-011-4
who? 20	Jean-Henri Fabre	979-11-5639-012-1
who? 21	Vincent van Gogh	979-11-5639-013-8
who? 22	Marie Curie	979-11-5639-014-5
who? 23	Henry David Thoreau	979-11-5639-015-2
who? 24	Andrew Carnegie	979-11-5639-016-9
who? 25	Coco Chanel	979-11-5639-017-6
who? 26	Charlie Chaplin	979-11-5639-018-3
who? 27	Ho Chi Minh	979-11-5639-019-0
who? 28	Ludwig van Beethoven	979-11-5639-020-6
who? 29	Mao Zedong	979-11-5639-021-3
who? 30	Kim Dae-jung	979-11-5639-022-0